OKAY, THEN TELL ME THE STORY AGAIN, PAPA.

THE STORY OF GREGORIO CORTEZ? AND ABOUT TEJANO AND CONJUNTO MUSIC?

YES, PLEASE! TELL IT!

WELL, GREGORIO WAS BORN ON A RANCH IN 1875...

NO! SING IT, TOO!

PATIENCE, SELENA. I HAVE TO SET THE STORY UP.

'KAY. HURRY!

MOVING FROM PLACE TO PLACE AS A RANCH HAND WAS A HARD LIFE, BUT HE FINALLY SETTLED IN KARNES COUNTY, TEXAS, IN 1900.

ON JUNE 12, 1901, SHERIFF MORRIS VISITED THE CORTEZ RESIDENCE LOOKING FOR A HORSE THIEF...

<THERE YOU GO. EAT UP.>*

*TRANSLATED FROM SPANISH.

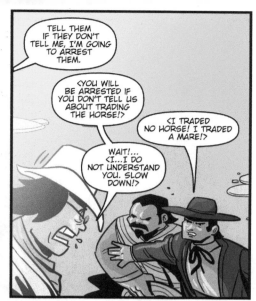

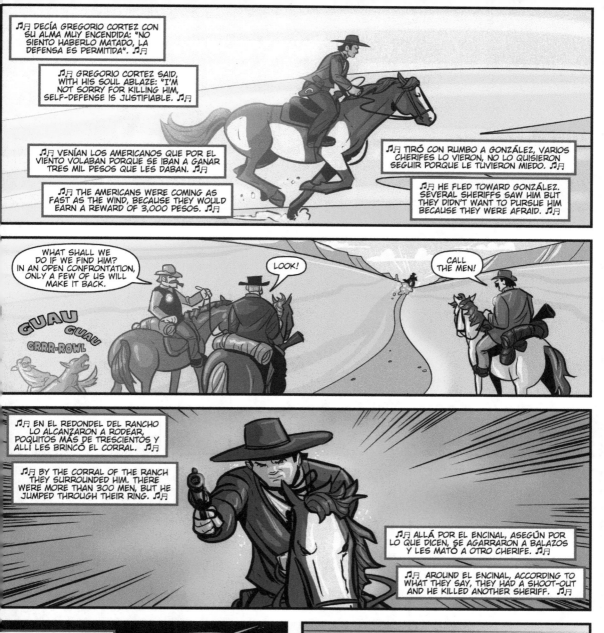

BE CALM, PRECIOSA!

BUT I KNOW WHAT HAPPENS, PAPA! THEY CAN'T CATCH HIM...HE HAS TO TURN HIMSELF IN BECAUSE HE'S SO FAST!

1976: CORPUS CHRISTI, TEXAS

IS THAT ALL YOU LEARNED? THAT CORTEZ WAS SOME KIND OF SUPERHERO?

ABRAHAM QUNITANILLA JR.! ARE YOU TELLING THAT TERRIBLE FOLKTALE AGAIN?

IT'S NOT TERRIBLE, MAMA. STORIES LIKE THAT ARE WHY WE HAVE TEJANO AND CONJUNTO MUSIC! I LOVE TEJANO!

SHE LOVES TEJANO! AND YOU SING IT SO WELL, PRECIOSA. BUT WHAT DID THE STORY TELL YOU?

THAT I SHOULD ALSO LEARN TO SPEAK SPANISH. BUT IT'S SO HARD!

BUT YOU SING IN SPANISH!

I BARELY KNOW WHAT I'M SAYING! I JUST LIKE THE SOUND OF IT WHEN I SING!

MY SILLY LITTLE SEL.

SO...WHAT KIND OF MUSIC HAS INFLUENCED TEJANO?

IT'S COUNTRY MUSIC, IT'S JAZZ, IT HAS ROOTS OF GERMAN POLKA, IT ALSO HAS MEXICAN MUSIC IN IT. I LIKE THE ACCORDION.

...

WHY THAT LOOK, PRECIOSA?

GRANDMA AND GRANDPA WERE FROM MEXICO. SO THAT MAKES YOU MEXICAN. MAMA IS HALF-MEXICAN AND HALF CHEROKEE INDIAN.

YES?

SO WHAT DOES THAT MAKE ME?

AMERICAN.

BUT THERE IS ANOTHER LESSON TO BE LEARNED HERE, SELENA.

WHAT LESSON, PAPA?

THAT GREAT THINGS COME FROM HUMBLE BEGINNINGS. THAT YOU MUST FIGHT FOR, AND DEFEND, WHAT YOU KNOW TO BE RIGHT IN YOUR HEART.

<AND NOW...I BRING YOU:>

SELENA Y LOS DINOS!

SUZETTE

ABRAHAM III

<"AIR SUPPLY"? IN SPANISH?>

<SURE, SURE, > ESE.

<MY SEL LOVES THEM, SO I TRANSLATED THE ->

<FOUR HOURS, RIGHT?>

SI. <ONE-HUNDRED DOLLARS. A BARGAIN.>

HA! <DON'T SPEND IT ALL IN ONE PLACE!>

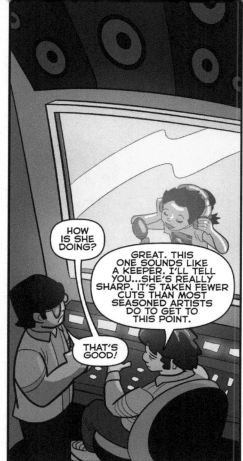

HOW IS SHE DOING?

GREAT. THIS ONE SOUNDS LIKE A KEEPER. I'LL TELL YOU...SHE'S REALLY SHARP. IT'S TAKEN FEWER CUTS THAN MOST SEASONED ARTISTS DO TO GET TO THIS POINT.

THAT'S GOOD!

STILL...

WHAT IS IT?

SHE'S SO... YOUNG. SO RAW.

THAT'S PART OF HER APPEAL.

WELL, I WAS TALKING WITH THE PRODUCER. WE THINK SHE'S NEEDS MORE... SEASONING.

I DON'T AGREE!

WE'LL FINISH THIS ALBUM OF COURSE. WE'LL PROBABLY RELEASE "SE ACABO AQUEL AMOR," MAYBE "TRES VECES NO," AND DEFINITELY "YA SE VA." YOU'LL GET SOME RADIO PLAY.

"SELENA, YOU KNOW I DON'T LIKE YOU DRESSING LIKE...THAT."

"LIKE WHAT, PAPA?"

"THAT! RUNNING ABOUT SHIRTLESS!"

"IT'S JUST A BRA! MY STYLE! MY SIGNATURE! PERHAPS I'LL... I'LL OPEN UP MY OWN SHOPS AND SELL THEM!"

"YOUR VOICE IS YOUR SIGNATURE, PRECIOSA."

"I JUST WANT THEM TO SEE YOU FOR WHO YOU ARE AND HEAR WHAT YOU CAN DO. NOT BLINDED BY...THOSE."

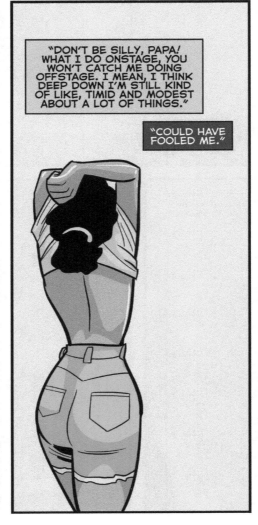

"DON'T BE SILLY, PAPA! WHAT I DO ONSTAGE, YOU WON'T CATCH ME DOING OFFSTAGE. I MEAN, I THINK DEEP DOWN I'M STILL KIND OF LIKE, TIMID AND MODEST ABOUT A LOT OF THINGS."

"COULD HAVE FOOLED ME."

"BUT ON STAGE, I RELEASE ALL THAT; I LET GO!"

NOW, I'M READY.

1988

CAN WE TRY THE REFRAIN AGAIN? I'M HAVING SOME DIFFICULTY IN THE THIRD MEASURE.

YEAH, HEARD THAT.

HA! GEE, THANKS.

KNOCK KNOCK!

I'D LIKE TO INTRODUCE YOU TO CHRIS PEREZ.

HEY.

CHRIS PLAYED WITH SHELLY LARES AND EVEN HAS HIS OWN BAND. I WANT TO HIRE HIM TO JOIN US.

CHRIS, THIS IS SUZETTE, ABRAHAM, AND OF COURSE, SELENA.

I'M CHRIS.

SELENA.

I KNOW.

I'M GLAD YOU KNOW.

OH, BROTHER.

OH SHUT UP.

"PRECIOSA! YOU CAN'T BE SERIOUS!"

"I AM, PAPA. THIS IS RIGHT. THIS IS REAL. FIRING HIM DIDN'T BREAK US UP. WE WERE FRIENDS FIRST, PAPA. I NEVER THOUGHT I'D WANT TO MARRY A MUSICIAN."

"I WILL FOLLOW WHAT MY HEART TELLS ME. AND IT TELLS ME THAT CHRIS IS THE ONE."

"THE...ONE. SEL, WHY MUST YOU ALWAYS BE SO STRONG-WILLED?"

"HMM...I WONDER WHERE I GET IT, PAPA?"

APRIL 2, 1992: NUECES COUNTY, TEXAS

MARCH 31, 1995: MIDNIGHT

‹IT'S OKAY...HOLD ON... I'M HERE.›

‹I'M HERE.›

"SO...THEY LEFT?"

RIGHT. I USUALLY DON'T LET HER LEAVE THE HOUSE WITHOUT KNOWING WHERE SHE WAS GOING, BUT I WAS ASLEEP.

YES, BUT AS HER HUSBAND, YOU NOTICED SHE'D LEFT?

I MEAN, I HEARD HER, BUT I DIDN'T WANT TO GET UP, YOU KNOW? I THOUGHT MAYBE SHE WAS GOING TO HANG OUT WITH MY DAD WHO HAD STAYED OVER THAT NIGHT.

I DIDN'T EVEN THINK TO ASK AND THEN... SHE WAS GONE.

I'M SORRY.

WHY DID THEY LEAVE THE HOTEL? I THOUGHT YOU FOUND –

WE'RE STILL PIECING THAT TOGETHER, BUT SELENA BELIEVED THAT...HER FORMER EMPLOYEE...HAD BEEN RAPED.

I DON'T UNDERSTAND... RAPED?

SHE TOLD SELENA SHE'D BEEN RAPED AND THAT THE PAPERS SHE INTENDED TO RETURN WERE IN HER CAR, WHICH WAS STOLEN.

SHE SAID NOTHING ABOUT IT WHEN WE WERE THERE EARLIER IN THE DAY. SHE STALLED US, CLEARLY LYING. SELENA AND I LEFT. BUT...SHE CALLED THAT NIGHT. I KNOW THAT... NOW.

COFFEE?

NO, THANK YOU. I'M CONFUSED. HOW DO YOU KNOW ABOUT SOME RAPE?

SELANA TOOK HER TO A HOSPITAL. THE RAPE KIT WAS NEGATIVE, SO SELENA RETURNED TO THE DAYS INN.

AND... AND THAT'S WHEN IT HAPPENED. WHY DIDN'T SHE BRING ME?

WE... PRESUME THAT THE RAPE STORY WAS A WAY TO GET SELENA TO COME ALONE.

31 DE MARZO: 11.45 A.M.

CLEANING SERVICE!

...

♫♪♫♫♪♫♫

♫♪♫♫♪♫♫

11:49 A.M.

BLAM!

WE BELIEVE SELENA WENT BACK TO THE MOTEL TO GET A...FABERGE EGG...A GIFT FROM HER EMPLOYEES THAT SHE HAD STOLEN.

YES. SELENA COLLECTS... COLLECTED...THIS IS JUST SO SENSELESS. IF SHE HAD NEEDED MONEY, SELENA WOULD'VE GIVEN IT HER.

THE DESK CLERK LOCKED THE LOBBY DOORS AND CALLED 911. BUT...IT WAS... TOO LATE.

"FINISH THE STORY, PAPA!"

"YOU FINISHED IT ALREADY, PRECIOSA. THE AUTHORITIES CAN'T CATCH HIM. BUT CORTEZ, FEELING ENOUGH BLOOD HAS BEEN SPILLED, TURNS HIMSELF IN."

"NO! YOU HAVE TO SING IT!"

♪♫ GREGORIO LE DICE A JUAN EN EL RANCHO DEL CIPRÉS: "PLATÍCAME QUÉ HAY DE NUEVO, YO SOY GREGORIO CORTEZ". ♪♫

♪♫ GREGORIO SAYS TO JUAN, AT THE RANCH OF THE CYPRESS: "TELL ME, WHAT'S NEW? I AM GREGORIO CORTEZ." ♪♫

♪♫ GREGORIO LE DICE A JUAN: "MUY PRONTO LO VAS A VER, ANDA HÁBLALE A LOS CHERIFES QUE ME VENGAN A APREHENDER". ♪♫

♪♫ GREGORIO SAYS TO JUAN: "YOU WILL SOON FIND OUT. GO AND CALL THE SHERIFFS, TELL THEM TO COME AND ARREST ME." ♪♫

♪♫ CUANDO LLEGAN LOS CHERIFES GREGORIO SE PRESENTÓ: "POR LAS BUENAS SI ME LLEVAN, PORQUE DE OTRO MODO NO". ♪♫

♪♫ WHEN THE SHERIFFS ARRIVED GREGORIO TURNED HIMSELF IN. "YOU CAN TAKE ME ONLY ON MY TERMS, NO OTHER WAY." ♪♫

♪♫ YA AGARRARON A CORTEZ, YA TERMINÓ LA CUESTIÓN, LA POBRE DE SU FAMILIA LA LLEVA EN EL CORAZÓN. ♪♫

♪♫ THEY CAUGHT CORTEZ AND THE CASE IS CLOSED. HIS POOR FAMILY IS ALWAYS IN HIS HEART. ♪♫

SEASIDE MEMORIAL PARK: CORPUS CHRISTI, TEXAS

♪♫ YA CON ESTA AHÍ ME DESPIDO CON LA SOMBRA DE UN CIPRÉS, AQUÍ SE ACABA CANTANDO LA TRAGEDIA DE CORTEZ. ♪♫

♪♫ I NOW TAKE MY LEAVE, BY THE SHADE OF A CYPRESS TREE. HERE I END SINGING THE TRAGEDY OF CORTEZ. ♪♫

TO DATE, SELENA QUINTANILLA-PEREZ HAS SOLD OVER 60 MILLION ALBUMS WORLDWIDE.

TIDALWAVE
COMICS

Michael L. Frizell ———————————————— Writer

Ramon Salas ———————————————— Art

Benjamin Glibert ———————————————— Letters

Darren G. Davis ———————————————— Editor

Joe Paradise ———————————————— Cover

Darren G. Davis
Publisher

Maggie Jessup
Publicity

Susan Ferris
Entertainment Manager

Steven Diggs Jr.
Marketing Manager

TIDALWAVE
PRODUCTIONS